T·H·E

"I Really Didn't Say

YOGI

Everything I Said!"

BOOK

by Yogi Berra

FOREWORD BY JOE GARAGIOLA • INTRODUCTION BY LARRY, TIM & DALE BERRA

WORKMAN PUBLISHING · NEW YORK

Library of Congress Cataloging-in-Publication Data

Berra, Yogi, 1925-
    The Yogi Book/by Yogi Berra.
    p.   cm.
    Includes bibliographical references
    ISBN 0-7611-1568-4
    1. Berra, Yogi, 1925- —Quotations. 2. Baseball players—
United States—Quotations. 3. Baseball managers—United
States—Quotations. 4. Baseball—United States—Quotations,
maxims, etc.
  I. Title
GV865.B4A32 1998   97-52802
796.357'092—dc21   CIP

Cover design by Paul Hanson
Book design by Paul Hanson and Elizabeth Johnsboen
Front cover and title page photo: Archive Photos
Back cover photo: Berra Family Collection

Workman books are available at special discounts when purchased
in bulk for premiums and sales promotions as well as for fund-
raising or educational use. Special editions or book excerpts can
be created to specification. For details, contact the Special Sales
Director at the address below.

Workman Publishing Company, Inc.
708 Broadway
New York, NY 10003-9555

Manufactured in the United States of America

First printing April 1999

10 9 8 7 6 5 4 3

DEDICATION

To my brothers, John (1), Mike (2), and Tony (3), and my sister, Josie (4), who convinced my parents, Pietro (5) and Paulina (6), to let me leave home and try to earn a living playing baseball.

To my sons, Larry, Tim, and Dale, and to the rest of the family for listening and remembering the sayings that I don't even know I say.

To my daughter-in-law Betsy, without whose efforts this book wouldn't have happened.

And finally, to my beautiful wife, Carmen, who tolerates me and for whom my love is unending.

FOREWORD

The Thrill From "The Hill"
by Joe Garagiola

My friend Yogi Berra and I began sharing our dreams when he was Lawdie and I was Joey, and we were just two baseball-playing youngsters growing up in the Italian-American section of St. Louis that was called "The Hill." These many years later, I'm asked if I'm surprised by all that Yogi went on to accomplish as a major league ballplayer, manager, and coach. I always answer no. Since we were kids, Yogi has been one of the most positive thinkers I have ever known and he's always been successful at everything that has interested him.

The arrow on the left is pointing to Joe; the one on the right is pointing to Yogi.

Yogi played in a record 14 World Series for the New York Yankees from 1947 to 1963; was voted the American League's Most Valuable Player in 1951, 1954, and 1955; ended his playing career with the most homers by a catcher in major league history; managed the Yankees to an American League pennant in 1964 and the New York Mets to a National

League pennant in 1973; and was elected to the Hall of Fame in 1972. He had a remarkable career. Yet it's funny that his lasting fame has come less from how he played and managed than from his unique way of speaking. Yogi is one of the most quoted people in the world.

Fans have labeled Yogi Berra "Mr. Malaprop," but I don't think that's accurate. He doesn't use the wrong words. He just puts words together in ways nobody else would ever do. You may laugh and shake your head when Yogi says something strange like, "It ain't over 'til it's over," but soon you realize that what he said actually makes perfect sense. And you find yourself using his words yourself because they are, after all, the perfect way to express a particular idea.

In fact, the key to Yogi-isms is Yogi's simple logic. He may take a different avenue than you would to get to where he's going, but it's the fastest, truest route. What you would say in a paragraph, he says in a sentence. If you say it in a sentence, Yogi needs only one word. If you use one word, Yogi just nods. Yogi's conversation is normal dialogue after taxes.

I've gotten lost more than once going to Yogi's house in New Jersey, so now I call for directions. Each time, I get a memorable response. A favorite is, "I know just where you are, Joey. You're not too far. But don't go the other way, come this way." Now, I've been accused of putting words in Yogi's mouth, but how could I make up a response like that? How can you improve on Yogi?

INTRODUCTION

To the Most Quoted Man
from Larry, Tim & Dale Berra

If we had a penny for every time we were asked what it was like to grow up with Yogi Berra as our father, we would probably own the world's largest pile of copper. It's certainly easy to recall the lineup of memorable events that most kids wouldn't have had the opportunity to experience: the times we played catch with Elston Howard in front of the dugout at Yankee Stadium; or got dunked in the clubhouse whirlpool by Mickey Mantle; or got patted on the head by Casey Stengel, as if we were favorite pets. But when we tell people about growing up as Yogi's sons, we always make it clear that to us everything seemed normal, even trips to the ballpark. That normalcy was a reflection of Dad.

So many times we have heard how difficult it was for someone growing up as the son or daughter of a celebrity. They had a tough time because the pressure was too great to live up to his or her legacy. As Yogi's sons, we never had that problem because our dad never acted like he was a celebrity. We have a famous father who prefers driving a Corvair to a Cadillac because it's more practical. Who treats the man who pumps his gas or sells him his newspaper as a good friend. And who makes the bed before leaving the house in the morning. It doesn't take much to make Dad happy. He finds joy in playing with his grandchildren, watching a good movie, or sinking a putt.

Because our father likes to keep life from becoming too complicated, he has made it an art to get to the root of any problem in about five seconds. Faced with the most complex equation, he will trim off the fat and, we marvel, come up with the easiest yet most profound—and quotable—solution imaginable. That he is able to do this is a gift. The three of us just haven't figured out what this gift is. No one has.

The person who might have the best idea is our mom, Carmen Berra, and she's not saying. Next to every great man is a great woman, and such is the case with Yogi and Carmen. Mom is intelligent and beautiful, as well as insightful. She had to be. How else could she have fallen for Dad? She knew what she was doing because they've been happily together for nearly fifty years. However, only Dad is responsible for Yogi-isms.

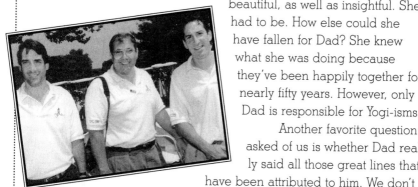

Left to right: Tim, Larry, and Dale

Another favorite question asked of us is whether Dad really said all those great lines that have been attributed to him. We don't know the sources of the numerous bogus Yogi-isms that are floating around, but we can tell you that the quotes included in this book are the real deal. Authentic Yogi Berra. Arlene Francis once asked Dad if he had read a biography someone had written about him and he replied, "Why should I? I was there." Well, we were there for Dad's classic Yogi-isms (and will be there for the future ones, too). We hope you enjoy them as much as we do!

"I really didn't say everything I said!"

This was a comment I made when someone asked me about quotes that I didn't think I said. Then again, I might have said 'em, but you never know.

Making speeches isn't for me. I'd rather the audience just asked me questions. But on Yogi Berra Day at Yankee Stadium in 1959, I overcame my nervousness to thank the fans. That's my son Larry on the right.

"Thank you for making this day necessary."

I think this was the saying that got it all started. Yogi Berra Day, 1947. I was being honored by my friends on The Hill in St. Louis.

Here I am with the Stags, the first team I played on as a kid. In the back (left to right) are Joe Garagiola, me, and Ben Pucci. Kneeling (left to right) are Charlie Riva and Johnny Columbo. This was taken at the Missouri Hall of Fame.

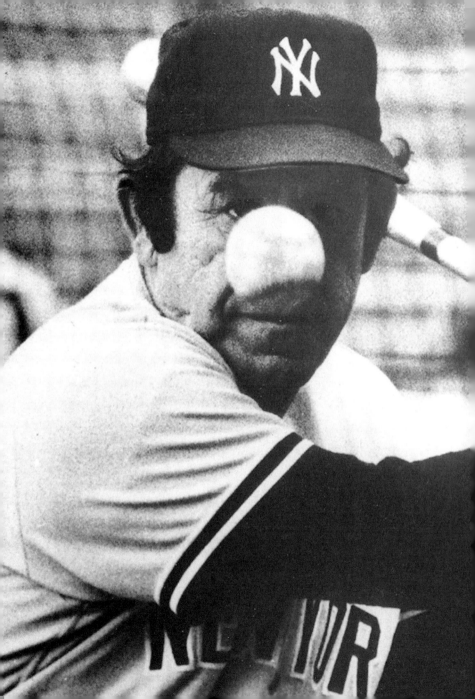

"You can't think and hit at the same time."

If you ask me, this is true with any sport. I said it in 1946 when I was with the Newark Bears playing Triple A. My manager told me not to swing at balls out of the strike zone. He said, "Yogi, next time you're up, think about what you're doing." I struck out in three pitches!

I could always see bad balls good. This ball looks like it saw me, too. At the time, I was a coach for the Yankees and knocking grounders to the infield before a game with Cleveland.

A few of the best came to a pre-season reunion in St. Petersburg. That's me with Eddie Lopat, Roger Maris, Casey Stengel, and Hank Bauer.

A writer asked me, "What makes a good manager?" I answered: **"Good players!"**

Whitey Ford says:

I've heard all the Yogi stories and have been involved in some, but when I think of Yogi, I realize there's so

Me and my buddy Whitey.

much to him—he has a great family, he's so honest, and helps his friends any way he can. The only bad thing I can say about Yogi is he never bought me a beer!

"Nobody goes there any-more. It's too crowded."

I was talking to Stan Musial and Joe Garagiola in 1959 about Ruggeri's restaurant in my old neighborhood in St. Louis. It was true!

I was maître d' at Ruggeri's for a couple of years in the '40s, during the off season. At that time, both Joe Garagiola and my brother John were waiters.

SERVICE

ICE CREAM DISHES

Cone or Cup	10¢
Large Cone or Cup	20¢
Floats	25¢
Sundaes	30¢
Thick Shakes	30¢
Pints	45¢
Banana Home Run	45¢
Quarts	85¢

SNACKS

Doughnut	5¢
Frankfurter	15¢
French Fries	15¢
Hamburger	25¢

In 1955, I did an opening for a snack bar in the Bronx. Despite what it looks like in this photo, I wasn't the only one to enjoy ice cream that day.

"**A** nickel ain't worth a dime anymore."

Who would doubt this? I notice it especially when I go to buy my papers in the morning at Henry's in Verona, New Jersey.

"The only reason I need these gloves is 'cause of my hands."

This is a doozie. Carm, Tim, and I were in the backyard gardening. I began complaining about getting scratches and mud all over my hands. Carmen really let me have it. She finally threw me a pair of gloves, and this was my reply.

No glove, see what happens—I got hit with a pitched ball during the 1952 World Series and broke my thumb.

Me: "**Where have you been?**"

Carmen: "**I took Tim to see _Doctor Zhivago._**"

Me: "**What the hell's wrong with him now?**"

Our game got rained out and I got home early. I was hungry.

When Tim played
football for the
University of
Massachusetts in the
early '70s, Carm and
I used to go up every
chance we got.

"We over- whelming underdogs."

I was reminiscing with Nolan Ryan one day about the 1969 Amazing Mets.

Nolan Ryan is soaking his hands in pickle juice pre-game— he said it prevented blisters! With him are Phil Linz and Kenny Boswell (with his head in the basket).

Nolan Ryan says:

If Yogi had gone to college, they would have made him talk clearer, but not better.

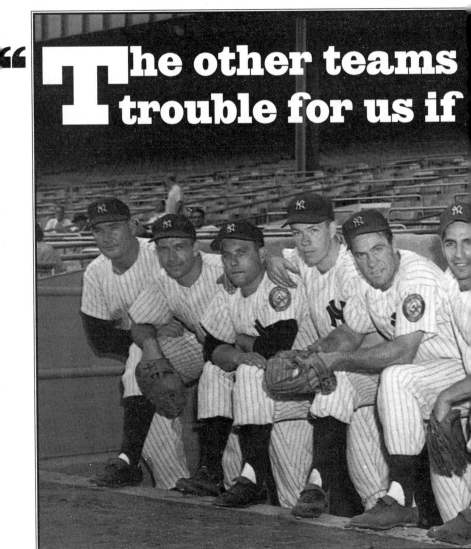

" **T**he other teams trouble for us if

Here we are before the opener of the 1952 World Series against the Dodgers (from left to right): Johnny Mize, Joe Collins, Gene Woodling, Gil McDougald, Hank Bauer, Phil Rizzuto, Billy Martin, Irv Noren, me, and Mickey Mantle. It doesn't get much better than this!

could make they win."

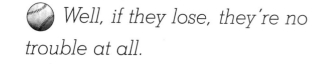 *Well, if they lose, they're no trouble at all.*

"It's never happened in World Series history, and it hasn't happened since."

This was the most exciting game I ever caught. Nobody talked about it in the dugout, not even Don and I. We couldn't— we were ahead by only two runs. I didn't know I was going to jump on Don until I jumped on him.

I was referring to the 1956 perfect game pitched by Don Larsen.

"It's déjà vu all over again!"

My comment after Mickey Mantle and Roger Maris hit back-to-back home runs for the umpteenth time. Makes perfect sense to me.

This picture was taken at a baseball clinic that was held in an armory in Manhattan. Gil Hodges, Phil Rizzuto, and Eddie Lopat were also there the day this photo was shot.

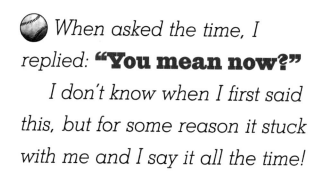 *When asked the time, I replied:* **"You mean now?"**

I don't know when I first said this, but for some reason it stuck with me and I say it all the time!

Here I am, clearing out my locker. My son Larry was obviously no help!

"We made too many wrong mistakes."

I said this after the 1960 World Series between the Yankees and Pirates. It was a seven-game series that ended when Bill Mazeroski hit the doggone home run over my head. There was no other way to explain how we ever lost that series.

As you can see by my face, we were in trouble!

"**If** people don't want to come to the ballpark, how are you going to stop them?"

Another close play for me at home plate. I'm putting the tag on Phillies shortstop Granny Hamner in the final game of the 1950 World Series.

⚾ Yes, I said this. I was talking to commissioner Bud Selig when attendance was down around the league. I think it was due to the threat of a strike.

"If you ask me a question I don't know, I'm not going to answer."

After a rough game, any questions seem like tough ones. Sometimes you just don't feel like talking about it. But like it or not, you have to face the press.

It was 1964, I was managing the Yankees, and the season opener with the Red Sox was one day away. I must have said something of note 'cause that guy on the left looks like he's trying to figure out how to interpret it.

So, after a difficult loss, I announced this to the writers before they had a chance to ask me a question.

I'm swinging away here! Hope it was a good one.

"Slump? I ain't in no slump... I just ain't hitting."

I never, ever thought I was in a slump. As far as I was concerned, tomorrow I was always going to get my hits, regardless of what I did today.

"It was hard to have a conversation with anyone, there were too many people talking."

I was at the *White House* for dinner by invitation of President Ford. Those politicians were so noisy, I couldn't hear a thing.

Gerald R. Ford says:

I was involved with a very special golf event in Vail, Colorado, for twenty years—The Jerry Ford Invitational. I recall one year on the thirteenth hole of the Vail Golf Club, Yogi's pants split. In perhaps what was the greatest nonverbal "Yogi-ism," the crowd roared when they realized he actually had on Yogi Bear undershorts.

I beat Julius Erving in a shoot-out at Beaver Creek, Colorado. He wasn't happy. Here, President Ford is giving me a congratulatory handshake.

*Playing golf one day,
I started to complain that my shot
was going to go into the water.
My friend Kevin Carroll said,
"Come on, Yogi, don't be like that.
Think positively." I replied:*

"Okay, I'm positive my shot is going into the water."

I recognize that look on my face. It's the one I get when a drive isn't headed where I'd like it to go. This time it was during an American Airlines Golf Classic. Hey, at least I have on a great outfit.

"**90%** of short putts don't go in."

I often practiced my putting in the living room. Larry and Tim should have paid more attention!

 So all right, they never go in!

"Why buy good luggage? You only use it when you travel."

That's Larry having a good time watching Carmen help me pack, back in the early days. Or should I say both of us were watching Carmen do the packing?

⚾ *My teammates were always ribbing me about my old luggage. You couldn't hurt my bags, but theirs could only get worse.*

"When you come to a fork in the road, take it."

I was giving Joe Garagiola directions from New York to our house in Montclair when I said this. Another time I was giving Joe directions and I told him, "I know just where you are. Don't go the other way, come this way." Joey has known me almost all my life. He always finds me.

The Stags, when
we were The Stags, the first team I played
for growing up in St. Louis. In the back (left to right): Ben Pucci,
Andrew (I forget his last name—we called him Nah Nah), and Charles (our
sponsor—he paid for our shirts). In the middle (left to right): Bob Berra (no
relation), Charlie Riva, me, and Paul Agusti. Sitting in front (left to right): Joe
Garagiola, George di Philippo, Pete Fansani, and Aldo Rossi.

I was voted into the Hall of Fame in 1972 and it was the greatest! Here I am on the big day in Cooperstown, New York. With me and my plaque are Joe Garagiola and Ed Stack, president of the Hall of Fame.

"**W**e're lost, but we're making good time!"

Casey Stengel and me in 1972 at the New York Press Photographers annual sports awards dinner.

I said this on the way to the Hall of Fame in Cooperstown in 1972. My wife, Carmen, and my sons, Larry, Tim, and Dale, were all in the car. Hard to believe it, but I got lost. Carmen was giving me a hard time, so I gave it back.

"If the world were perfect, it wouldn't be."

I believe you have to take the good with the bad, otherwise how do you know when things are good? If the world were perfect, how would you know?

The umpire called me out on strikes here. I guess I was a little upset.

I was receiving the key to New York City on a miserably hot and humid day. Mayor Lindsay's wife, Mary, commented on how cool I looked, and I replied:

"You don't look so hot yourself."

I guess I was a little nervous about the speech I had to make.

*See? I was in style
way back when.*

Mickey and me on opening day in 1956.

During an interview, Bryant Gumbel told me he wanted to do some word association. The first thing he said was: "Mickey Mantle." I replied: **"What about him?"**

Phil Rizzuto says:

Of all the Yogi Berra stories I know (and I know quite a few), there is one that is my favorite. Yogi and Carmen invited my wife, Cora, and me to see their new home in Montclair, New Jersey. After having a tour, my reaction was: "Wow, Yogi! What a beautiful mansion you've got here!" Yogi replied: "What do you mean, Phil? It's nothing but a bunch of rooms."

Phil Rizzuto and I played a lot of cards when we traveled. Phil was a great shortstop, but a lousy card player.

A reporter asked me, "What would you do if you found a million dollars?" I replied:

"I'd see if I could find the guy that lost it, and if he was poor, I'd give it back."

My parents always taught me to be honest. I figured if someone lost that much money, he'd be broke.

Me with my father, Pietro, and mother, Paulina. My mom made great coffee. Really strong. It would grow hair on your chest.

"If I didn't wake up I'd still be sleeping."

I had set my alarm and it didn't go off. Man, was I relieved that I woke up on time.

This was taken during a barn-storming trip to Japan in the 1950s. At the end of the season, the Japanese invited players from the U.S. to compete against their teams. We had a ball.

"I usually take a two-hour nap from 1 to 4."

Carmen and I were on our way back from one of our trips to Japan. I guess my nap was out of the question.

Life on the road could get kind of crazy, so it helped me to have a routine. All of my career, I would wake up, eat breakfast, go for a walk, come back and read the paper, have a little lunch, and then take my two-hour nap—from 1 to 4.

"If you can't imitate him, don't copy him."

I said this when I was with the New York Mets. During batting practice one day, I was leaning up against the cage and overheard Ron Swoboda saying that he wanted to hit like the great Hall of Famer Frank Robinson. Ron was trying to stand up close to the plate like only Frank could do, daring you to throw it in on him.

Just me being a ham.

"It gets late early out there."

Left field in Yankee Stadium was tough to play during the late autumn. World Series time! The shadows would creep up on you and you had a tough time seeing the ball off the bat. Everyone knew what I meant . . . I think.

Me and Yankee Stadium right before my managerial debut in the 1964 opener with Boston.

I was asked, "Yogi, when you were young, what did you like best about school?" I answered: **"When it's closed."**

I've been asked that question a lot, and I always give the same answer. I guess I drove the teachers crazy when I was a kid. I begged my mom and pop for years to let me quit and go to work. In those days, things were different. I wanted to work and help my family.

*This was taken during
a 1942 American
Legion game in
Hastings, Nebraska.
That's Gene Mauch on
the right, catching.*

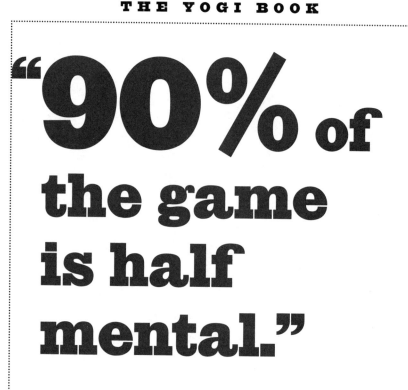

"90% of the game is half mental."

🏐 *I have said this many times. It's one of my better coaching tips.*

I'm giving good advice, I hope, at a Little League clinic that was held at Yankee Stadium.

*Just a
bunch of us killing time on
the train. Standing (left to right): Joe Page,
Eddie Lopat, and Ralph Houk. Sitting (left to right): Tommy
Henrich, me, Allie Reynolds, and Sherm Lollar.*

While playing a game of twenty questions, I asked:

"Is he living?"
"Is he living now?"

People still rib me about this one. We used to play twenty questions or cards to pass the time on train trips. This particular time, I was playing with Del Webb, then part owner of the Yankees.

"Always go to other people's funerals, otherwise they won't go to yours."

Mickey and I had been talking about all the funerals we'd been to in that one year. We were saying that pretty soon there would be no one left to come to ours.

Maybe Mickey and I were pointing this out to restaurateur Toots Shor during one of our many visits to our favorite night spot.

"Steve McQueen looks good in this movie. He must have made it before he died."

Carm and I with the boys and our cocker spaniel, Taffy.

After Christmas dinner, Carmen, Larry, Tim, Dale, and I were sitting in the den watching Papillon. Come on now—I was half asleep—you know what I meant.

My movie debut,
with Doris Day and Cary Grant no
less. That's Roger Maris and Mickey Mantle on either
side of Doris. I'm next to Cary.

"I'm as red as a sheet."

 *You may not know that I appeared in the movie* That Touch of Mink *with Cary Grant and Doris Day. You'd think I'd be used to embarrassing moments after playing big league games in front of so many people. But after flubbing my line during the movie shoot, I flubbed the apology, too.*

I was a movie critic for a while and was asked if the movie Fatal Attraction *had frightened me. I remarked:* **"Only the scary parts."**

This was the logo used when I was a movie critic. It was drawn by Tom Villante, who used to be a bat boy for the Yankees.

©1987, Tom Villante Marketing inc.

I'm dishing out my special spaghetti at a sports celebrity luncheon held in Los Angeles as a charity fund-raiser.

After seeing the opera Tosca, Carmen and I were on our way back to the hotel. She asked me what I thought and I replied:

"I really liked it. Even the music was good."

Carmen has never let me live this one down.

When asked if I wanted my pizza cut into four or eight slices, I replied: **"Four. I don't think I can eat eight."**

Roger Maris, Mickey Mantle, Mickey's wife, Marilyn, and me on the bus to somewhere. Probably on the way to a meal. We always went out to eat together. Get a load of Mickey's hat!

*It must have been
a good day. Look
at that smile.*

"I wish I had an answer to that, because I'm tired of answering that question."

The Yankees weren't doing well and day after day I was asked why. I truly didn't have an answer, but I sure wish I did. When I came up with this reply, all the reporters said, "You said one again, Yogi!"

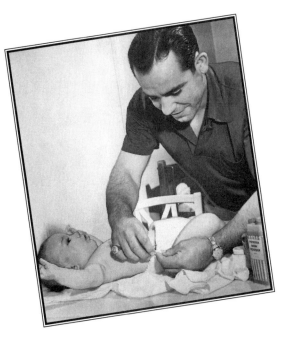 *We were shooting the breeze in the clubhouse when the subject of having insurance came up. My response was:* **"I don't know what the best type is, but I know none is bad."**

Most people I know still argue which kind to buy.

This shot of me with my son Larry was definitely set up. I didn't change diapers. Well, occasionally, but only when they were wet.

This photo was taken in my office at the bowling alley that Phil Rizzuto and I owned from the late '50s to the mid '60s. It was a landmark on Route 3 in New Jersey, just west of New York City.

When Max Nicholas, then head of Yankee public relations, called, I sleepily answered the phone. "Sorry, Yogi," he said. "I hope I didn't wake you." I replied: **"Nah, I had to get up to answer the phone anyway."**

From the early '50s to the '60s, I worked for Yoo-Hoo and enjoyed sampling the goods.

At a Yoo-Hoo convention, a woman asked me, "Is Yoo-Hoo hyphenated?" I responded:

"No ma'am, it isn't even carbonated!"

"**P**air up in threes."

Dale and me after he was acquired by the Yankees from the Pirates. He was the first major leaguer to play full-time on a team managed by his father. I'm a very proud papa.

During spring training at the Ft. Lauderdale stadium, I was making the players do wind sprints after a tough loss. I was looking at Dave Righetti, Bob Shirley, and my son Dale when I said this.

Jack Buck at the mike, calling a Cardinals game.

 *After doing a radio show with Jack Buck in St. Louis, a check was handed to me made out to "Pay to Bearer." I turned to Jack and said:* **"You've known me all this time and you still can't spell my name!"**

With Johnny Bench catching, it was no wonder we lost to the Reds four straight in 1976.

"**Congratulations. I knew the record would stand until it was broken.**"

I sent this in a telegram to Johnny Bench after he broke my record for most home runs by a catcher.

"**D**on't get me right, I'm just asking!"

 *I was negotiating a new contract with Yankee owner Dan Topping. We didn't have agents back then and I didn't want to insult him.*

Here I am in 1963 signing on to manage the Yankees. With me are general manager Ralph Houk (left) and co-owner Dan Topping (standing).

I think the expression on my face says it all. I couldn't have been more pleased than when I signed my contract to become the Yankee manager in 1963.

"Never answer an anonymous letter."

This isn't as bad as it sounds. Some letters do have return addresses with no name, you know.

"You can observe a lot by watching."

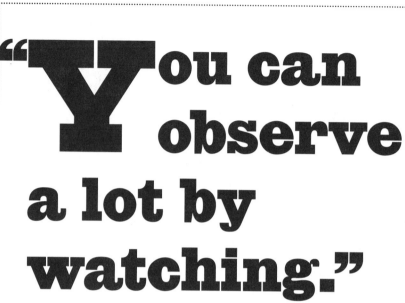

🔵 *I was managing the Yankees in 1964 when I said this. I yelled it to the players, who were not paying attention to the game.*

Managing is very stressful, sometimes downright nerve-racking. Here I am in an obvious nail-biter.

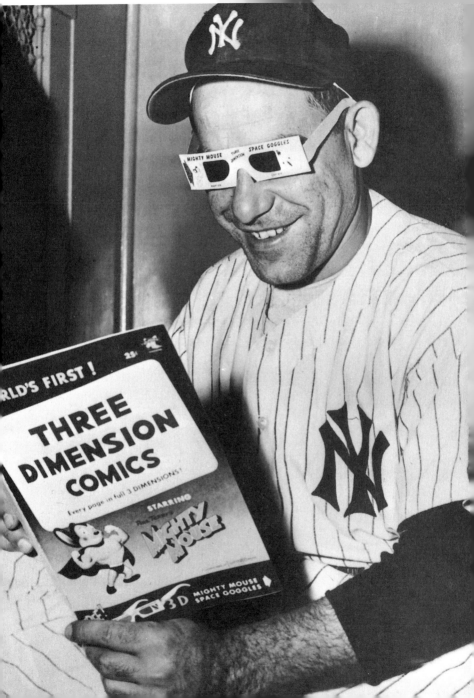

My roommate Bobby Brown was studying to become a doctor. I was well known for my avid comic book reading. One night, Bobby looked up from reading his anatomy textbook and asked me how my comic book turned out. I said: **"Great, and how did yours come out?"**

My good buddies Bobby Brown and Tommy Byrne (the toughest pitcher I every caught) during the 1952 World Series against the Dodgers.

My favorite pastime back then.

 When I was managing the New York Yankees, a reporter asked if Don Mattingly had exceeded his expectations this season. I replied: **"I'd say he's done more than that."**

Don Mattingly says:

What sticks in my mind the most is Yogi's comment about all the batting practice I used to take. "Don," he said, "you're going to hit yourself right into a slump."

The day this photo was taken in 1984, Don got four hits in a game against the Detroit Tigers. One of my favorite people, Don ended the year with a .343 batting average and the AL batting championship.

"It's not too far, it just seems like it is."

Taking in the sights in Japan on one of our off-season barnstorming trips.

I am the absolute worst at directions, or so I'm told. I was trying to tell someone how to get to our old racquetball club.

Here I am signing my quota of balls for the day.

🔵 When I was told that a Jewish mayor was elected in Dublin, Ireland, I responded: **"Only in America!"**

What can I say? Geography was never my strong point.

"**Y**ou've got to be careful if you don't know where you're going 'cause you might not get there!"

SCORE
BOYS + GIRLS
3 + 0

I'm not sure it was
my goal to wind up
with three sons, but
here I am with my
third, Dale.

*If you don't set goals, you
can't regret not reaching them.*

When a reporter asked me if Joe DiMaggio was fast, I answered: **"No, he just got there in time."**

Joe and I were in the club-house celebrating our 1951 World Series win.

During an interview, Arlene Francis asked me if I had read my new book, Yogi: It Ain't Over... I said: **"No, I was there."** *Well, I was.*

Why shouldn't I look happy here? We had a one-game advantage over the A's in the 1973 World Series.

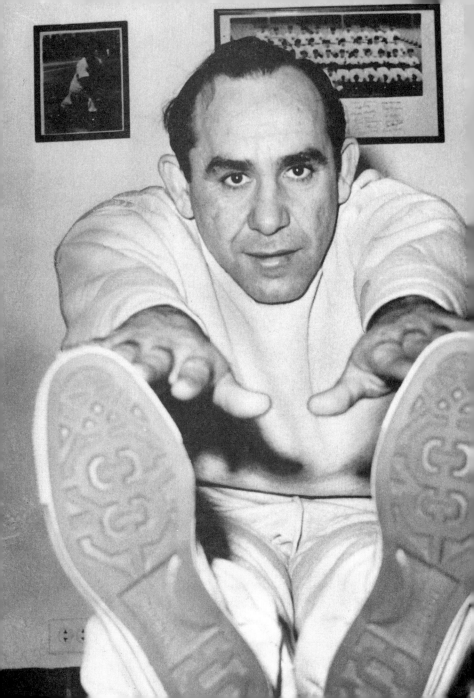

When asked, "Yogi, what size cap do you want?" I replied:

"I don't know. I'm not in shape yet."

Every spring we would get fitted for new uniforms. It's a big ordeal and pretty boring. Once in a while, I can come up with a joke. This one I'm still hearing about.

This was taken at my home in the winter. I'm really not in shape yet—can't seem to get to my toes!

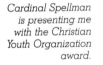 *When I returned home from Italy, Cardinal Spellman asked me if I had had an audience with the Pope. I said, "No, but I saw him." Then I was asked what I had said to His Holiness. I couldn't remember exactly, but he said, "Hello, Yogi," and I responded:*

"Hello, Pope."

Cardinal Spellman is presenting me with the Christian Youth Organization award.

Looking up, but I doubt that I have the weather on my mind.

When I was coaching with the Houston Astros, Marc Hill, Gene Clines, and I were on our way to play golf. I was in the backseat of the car, and all at once it started to rain. I asked: **"Where's that coming from?"**

Those two wanted to call the networks to tell them what I had said!

My kids would take turns coming to games with me and sitting in the dugout. Here Larry joins me during a Mets game.

We were going to have some of our blinds repaired, only I didn't know it. I was upstairs when my son Larry called out, "Dad, the guy is here for the venetian blinds." I told him:

"Look in my pants pocket and give him five bucks."

*I look like Hannibal
Lecter here.*

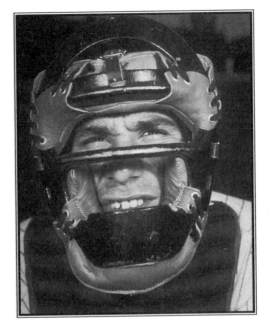

🔵 *In the dugout, someone said
to me, "Yogi, you're ugly," and I
said:* **"So? I don't hit with
my face."**

*Razzing and ribbing takes
place all the time in baseball. The
visiting team dugouts really gave
it to me, so I had to give it back.*

While speaking with writers before the 1973 playoffs about the Cincinnati "Big Red Machine," I said: **"Tony Perez is a big clog in their machine."**

Here's Tony at bat in 1973, at Shea Stadium. Although I never got to play against him, I had a lot of opportunities to watch him play. He's a nice guy and was a helluva clutch hitter.

*Me and Carm
cutting a rug at Grossinger's, a one-
time popular resort in the Catskills.*

"We have a good time together, even when we're not together."

This just slipped out when someone asked me about my beautiful wife.

"Little League baseball is a good thing 'cause it keeps the parents off the streets

and the kids out of the house!"

I was giving the Pinehurst Lions Club team a few pointers here.

Maybe this should be the other way around. All kidding aside, I do think Little League can be a great experience for kids, but it should be fun!

"The future used to be."

I just meant that times are different. Not necessarily better or worse. Just different.

ain't what it

Mickey Mantle, me, Whitey Ford, Joe DiMaggio, and Casey Stengel got together at Yankee Stadium before an Old Timers Game in 1974.

*Buddy
Harrelson was called
out trying to score in the tenth inning of
the second game of the 1973 World Series. As good an
umpire as Augie Donatelli was, he got this one wrong—and I let him know it!*

"It ain't over 'til it's over!"

That was my answer to a reporter when I was managing the New York Mets in July 1973. We were about nine games out of first place. We went on to win the division.

Putting It All Together:
Words of Inspiration From Yogi

This is an excerpt from the Commencement speech I delivered when I received my doctorate from Montclair State University in 1996.

Just call me Dr. Berra.

A lot of people have been quoting me ever since I came to play for the Yankees in 1946. But, as I once said, I really didn't say everything I said. So now it's my turn. I want to give some of my famous advice to the graduates.

First: Never give up, because it ain't over 'til it's over.

Second: During the years ahead, when you come to a fork in the road, take it.

Third: Don't always follow the crowd, because nobody goes there anymore. It's too crowded.

Fourth: Stay alert—you can observe a lot by watching.

Fifth and last: Remember that whatever you do in life, 90 percent of it is half mental.

In closing, I want to quote myself again: Thank you, Montclair State University, for making this day necessary.

My pride
and joy—
they made
this book
necessary.

Yogi

Apples Don't Fall Far From the Tree

1. Carmen: **"I need to go shopping for clothes to shop in."**
2. Larry: **"You can't lose if you win."**
3. Tim: **"I knew exactly where it was, I just couldn't find it."**
4. Dale: **"The similarities between my father and me are different."**
5. Betsy: **"Sometimes you have to get lost to find yourself."**
6. Carla: **"I'm so hungry right now, I can't even look at food."**
7. Lindsay: **"The water is cold until you get wet."**
8. Larry Jr.: **"This is very poorly unorganized."**
9. Gretchen: **"Grammy has so many clothes, she never wears the same outfit once."**
10. Bridgette: **"Shut up and talk."**
11. Whitney: **"How can I find it if it's lost?"**
12. Christopher: **"I eat apples, but not fruit."**
13. Andrew: **"I don't remember leaving, so I guess we didn't go."**
14. Maria: **"I double checked it six times."**
15. Nicholas: **"I'm hiding these right here!"**

PHOTO CREDITS

I'm camping out under a pop foul, ready to make the catch. Notice the perfect form!

Page 3: Daily News, L.P. New York

Page 4: National Baseball Library & Archive Photo Collection

Page 7: Berra Family Collection

Page 8: The New York Times

Page 11: Sporting News/Archive Photos

Page 12: AP/Wide World Photos

Page 14: AP/Wide World Photos

Page 15: Cleveland Press/Everett Collection

Page 17: UPI/Corbis-Bettmann

Page 18: AP/Wide World Photos

Page 21: AP/Wide World Photos

Page 23: Berra Family Collection

Page 25: UPI/Corbis-Bettmann

Page 26–27: AP/Wide World Photos

Page 28: AP/Wide World Photos

Page 31: Daily News, L.P.

Page 32: Berra Family Collection

Page 35: Berra Family Collection

Page 36–37: AP/Wide World Photos

Page 39: AP/Wide World Photos

Page 40: Everett Collection

Page 43: Berra Family Collection

Page 45: Cleveland Press/Everett Collection

Page 46: Bob Olen/Berra Family Collection

Page 47: Bob Gilman/Berra Family Collection

Page 49: Sporting News/Archive Photos

Page 50: Berra Family Collection

Page 51: Cleveland Press/Everett Collection

Page 53: AP/Wide World Photos

Page 54–55: Berra Family Collection

Page 56: AP/Wide World Photos

Page 57: Daily Mirror/Corbis

Page 58: National Baseball Library & Archive Photo Collection/Bettmann Archive

Page 60: National Baseball Library & Archive Photo Collection/ Bettmann Archive

Page 61: National Baseball Library & Archive Photo Collection/Bettmann Archive

Page 62: Archive Photos

Page 65: Daily News, L.P. New York

Page 67: Sporting News/Archive Photos

Page 68: National Baseball Library & Archive Photo Collection

Page 70: UPI/Corbis-Bettmann

Page 72: Bill Mark/Berra Family Collection

Page 75: National Baseball Library & Archive Photo Collection

Page 78: Tom Villante Marketing Inc.

Page 79: Berra Family Collection

Page 81: National Baseball Library & Archive Photo Collection

Page 82: AP/Wide World Photos

Page 84: Cleveland Press/Everett Collection

Tim and Larry give me a hand keeping some of my trophies in top form.

It ain't over yet!